W9-CHK-852

Earthforms

Plains

by Christine Webster

Consultant:
Robert S. Anderson, PhD
Associate Professor of Geological Sciences
University of Colorado at Boulder

Capstone
press

Mankato, Minnesota

Bridgestone Books are published by Capstone Press,
151 Good Counsel Drive, P.O. Box 669, Mankato, Minnesota 56002.
www.capstonepress.com

Library of Congress Cataloging-in-Publication Data
Webster, Christine.
    Plains / by Christine Webster.
        p. cm.—(Bridgestone books. Earthforms)
    Includes bibliographical references (p. 23) and index.
    ISBN 0-7368-3715-9 (hardcover)
    1. Plains—Juvenile literature. I. Title. II. Series.
GB572.W43 2005
910'.914'5—dc22   2004014283

Summary: Describes plains, including how they form, plants and animals on plains, how people and
    weather change plains, plains in North America, and the West Siberian Plain.

Editorial Credits
Becky Viaene, editor; Juliette Peters, designer; Anne McMullen, illustrator; Wanda Winch,
    photo researcher; Scott Thoms, photo editor

Photo Credits
Bruce Coleman Inc./L. Veisman, 18
Corbis/Annie Griffiths Belt, 16; Ted Spiegel, 6; Terry W. Eggers, cover
James P. Rowan, 4, 12
Minden Pictures/Jim Brandenburg, 10
Photodisc/B. Drake, 1; Photolink/D. Falconer, 14
Steve Mulligan, 8

1 2 3 4 5 6 10 09 08 07 06 05

Table of Contents

What Are Plains?

Plains are nearly flat areas of land. They often have small, rolling hills. Most areas on a plain are about the same height.

Plains are different sizes. Some cover only a few acres. Others cover millions of acres.

Three types of plains are found on earth. Floodplains form near rivers. Coastal plains are found along oceans. Inland plains have land on all sides.

◄ Sunflowers bloom on Nebraska's plains. These plains are part of North America's Great Plains.

How Do Plains Form?

Glaciers, rivers, and oceans all form plains. Long ago, large sheets of ice called glaciers moved across the land. They flattened the land and formed inland plains.

Today, plains are formed by rivers and oceans. Rivers can overflow their normal banks. Later, they dry up and leave mud and sand behind. The mud and sand form a floodplain.

Ocean waves make coastal plains. They push sand to new areas. Over time, waves level out the sand.

◄ The Arkansas River overflows its banks. It washes mud and sand into new areas to create floodplains.

Plants on Plains

Climate affects plant life on plains. The Great Plains is an inland plain with different climates. In cold, northern areas thick pine forests grow. In warm, dry areas, short buffalo grass and tall Indian grass grow.

Africa's Bangweulu Floodplains have a hot climate. Many types of grass, including papyrus grass, grow on these plains.

The coastal plains in Florida have a warm, wet climate. Cypress, water oak, and ash trees grow on these plains.

◀ Kansas' warm climate helps Indian grass grow up to 7 feet (2.1 meters) tall.

Animals on Plains

Many animals make their homes on plains. Antelopes, coyotes, and prairie dogs live on the Great Plains. This inland plain was once home to millions of bison. Today, few bison are left.

Many animals live on floodplains. Beavers, river otters, and raccoons make floodplains their home.

Coastal plains are also home to many animals. Elk, bears, and fox are found on these plains.

◄ On the plains, a prairie dog peeks out of its home. Not far away, bison eat grass and lie in dirt to keep cool.

Weather Changes Plains

Stormy weather can affect plant life on plains. In summer, thunderstorms form over plains. During a thunderstorm, lightning can strike dry grasslands and start fires. These wildfires burn everything in their paths. Often tornadoes race across plains. Their strong winds destroy plants and homes.

Hot, dry weather can also affect plants growing on plains. Without enough rain, plants die. Cracks form in the soil. Dry soil sometimes blows away.

◀ Dry weather leaves mud cracks and few plants on some plains. Weather can ruin large areas of plains.

People Change Plains

Farming and building have changed the natural state of plains. Plains have rich dirt for growing crops. Farmers also raise cattle on plains. People build roads and houses on plains. Crops and buildings now stand where **native** plains animals and plants once lived.

Hunting has lowered the number of animals on the plains. At one time, millions of bison roamed the plains. Today, only about 200,000 are left.

◄ Crop fields cover the Great Plains. The Great Plains covers a huge area of land, but few people live there.

Plains in North America

The Great Plains is in North America. It spreads from central Canada through the United States.

The Great Plains covers 1.1 million square miles (2.9 million square kilometers). The area is covered mostly with dry grassland. People farm on this huge inland plain.

People also farm on the plains of northwest Honduras. Bananas grow well in this coastal plain's tropical climate.

◀ Large amounts of wheat and corn are grown on the Great Plains.

West Siberian Plain

Russia's West Siberian Plain is one of the world's largest plains. It lies between the Ural Mountains and the Yenisei River. This plain covers at least 1.2 million square miles (3 million square kilometers).

Farmers grow many different crops on the West Siberian Plain. Buckwheat is the most common. Wheat, sunflowers, and barley grow there too. Farmers also raise cattle, reindeer, and sheep on this plain.

◄ Some of the world's largest floodplains form near the Yenisei River on the West Siberian Plain.

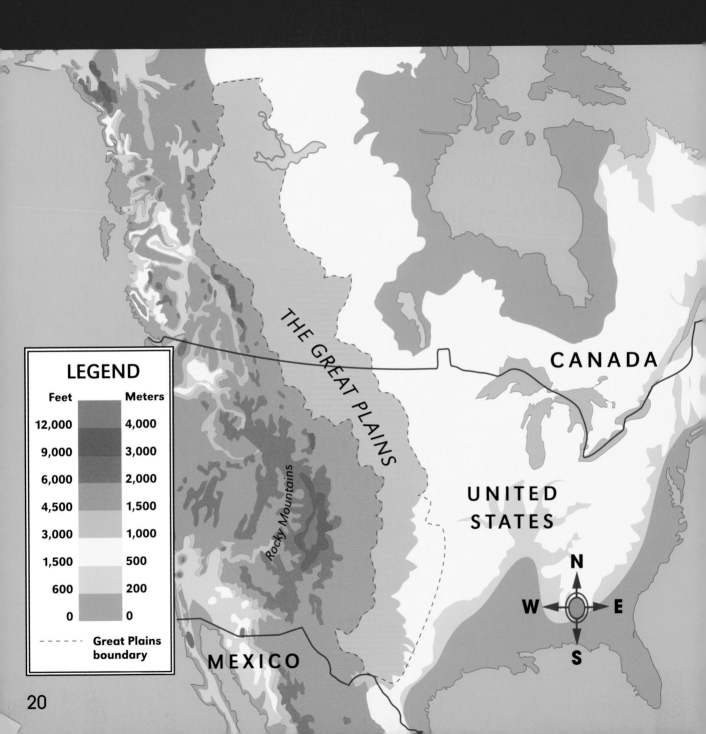

LEGEND

Feet		Meters
12,000		4,000
9,000		3,000
6,000		2,000
4,500		1,500
3,000		1,000
1,500		500
600		200
0		0

- - - Great Plains
boundary

THE GREAT PLAINS

Rocky Mountains

CANADA

UNITED
STATES

MEXICO

N
W   E
S

Plains on a Map

On an **elevation** map, different colors show different elevations. On this map, the Great Plains is shown as almost flat.

Plains can also be seen on **relief maps**. Relief maps are models showing earth's surface as flat and raised areas. Plains have low relief and are almost flat on these maps.

Look for a plain on a map. Is the plain near an ocean or river? Use these clues to decide if the plain is a coastal, flood, or inland plain.

◄ This elevation map shows the Great Plains as a nearly level area east of the Rocky Mountains.

Glossary

climate (KLYE-mit)—the usual weather in a place

elevation (el-uh-VAY-shuhn)—the height above sea level; sea level is defined as zero elevation.

glacier (GLAY-shur)—a huge moving body of ice found in mountain valleys or polar regions

native (NAY-tiv)—a person, animal, or plant that originally lived or grew in a certain place

relief map (ri-LEEF MAP)—a map that uses shading or a raised surface to show areas of high or low ground

Read More

Bradley, Catherine. *Life on the Plains.* World Book Ecology. Chicago: World Book, 2001.

Whitehouse, Patricia. *Plains.* My World of Geography. Chicago: Heinemann Library, 2005.

Internet Sites

FactHound offers a safe, fun way to find Internet sites related to this book. All of the sites on FactHound have been researched by our staff.

Here's how:
1. Visit *www.facthound.com*
2. Type in this special code **0736837159** for age-appropriate sites. Or enter a search word related to this book for a more general search.
3. Click on the **Fetch It** button.

FactHound will fetch the best sites for you!

Index